Tigress Weeps,

Angels Dream

Musings of Maranatha

Mara Root

Preface

Welcome to *"Tigress Weeps, Angels Dream"*

Step into a realm where poetry breathes life into the powerful dance of our inner worlds, intertwining raw vulnerability with celestial dreams. This collection invites you to explore the depths of your soul, revealing the fierce strength within and the ethereal aspirations that guide us toward our divine purpose.

Tigress Weeps

Within the heart of a warrior, strength intertwines with tears, a fierce soul, unafraid to cry, revealing power through vulnerability. Guarding art with tender might, hiding magnificence within, the Tigress roars in silent grace, her tears, a testament to strength.

Angels Dream

An innocent spirit whispers dreams, sacred visions of purity and hope, longing to remain unseen, Yet destined to shine with divine light. Dreams of angels, pure and true, reflecting heavenly desires, guiding the spirit to its destiny, unveiling purpose in celestial hues.

Tigress Weeps, Angels Dream

This collection speaks not of battle, but of an extraordinary union, soul and spirit, hand in hand, transcending earthly realms. Even in moments of despair, the heavens hear our cries, guiding us to our divine calling, with a touch of the ethereal. A celebration of faith and flesh, harmony in every verse, each poem, a luminous gem, illuminating paths of spiritual growth. Prepare to be enchanted, for this collection reveals the soul's most profound truths, a dance of destiny and bliss.

Illuminations from Literary Giants

"To realize one's destiny is a person's only real obligation."
— Paulo Coelho, *The Alchemist* (1988) (Author of *The Alchemist*, renowned for his spiritual and philosophical novels.)

"Out of suffering have emerged the strongest souls; the most massive characters are seared with scars."
— Kahlil Gibran, *The Prophet* (1923) (Author of The Prophet, celebrated for his poetic and mystical writings)

Divine Love:
"This Path to God
Made me such an old sweet beggar.
I was starving until one night
My love tricked God Himself
To fall into my bowl."
— Hafez, *The Subject Tonight Is Love* (translated by Daniel Ladinsky)(Beloved Persian poet, known for his lyrical poetry and spiritual themes)

"Let yourself be silently drawn by the strange pull of what you really love. It will not lead you astray."
— Rumi, *Rumi: Unseen Poems* (translated by Brad Gooch and Maryam Mortaz, 2019)(Beloved poet and Sufi mystic, renowned for his profound spiritual insights.)

Introduction

Once upon a time, in a teen's heart, shadows of depression played hide and seek. My father, a beacon of light, nudged me to write, transforming my journal into a secret garden. Instead of prose, my thoughts blossomed into poetry, revealing an unexpected talent.

Naturally reserved, sharing these poems is an act of daring vulnerability. In a world where mental health was hush-hush, I wore a mask. My early poems, dark yet witty, were silent screams. I even published anonymously, craving the freedom to express myself without restraint.

Over time, my poetry evolved, mirroring my journey to strength and empowerment. Initially, I crafted poems like a jeweler, each word a gem. Now, my writing flows like a river, spontaneous and inspired, as if whispered by an angel.

Poetry is my vacation, a place of wonder and discovery. Unlike lengthy books, poetry is a pocket-sized adventure, capturing universal emotions in a few lines. It's like carrying a piece of magic anywhere, anytime. Plus, it's much lighter than lugging around a novel!

This collection is extraordinary, representing my spiritual journey. Through poetry, I connect with the divine, both outside and within. It's a joyful escape, allowing me to express desires without shame and find solace in faith. This book is a vessel of light, a testament to the power of art as a path to spiritual growth and self-discovery. And hey, it's cheaper than therapy!

Acknowledgments

I would like to begin by expressing my deepest gratitude to my father, Richard Root, my first teacher and eternal guide. Your unwavering support and wisdom have been my foundation. From letting me join your college classes as a child to encouraging me to revise your students' papers, you always believed in my potential. You taught me to scurry after lizards, catch them, and hang them on my shirt, climb the tallest trees, pick the best blackberries along the river banks, and face the roaring ocean without fear. You showed me how to paint, not just for skill, but for emotional release and the joy of embracing the limitless chaos of one's mind on the canvas.

Our conversations, filled with wonder and Jim Carrey humor, have shaped my understanding of love and life. Some of my favorite memories are of you reading the Italian folklore book your dad gifted to Gianna and me every night, making pizzas from scratch, and speeding along Mt. Baldy in your Jaguar when Gianna screamed at you to slow down but you listened to my little rascal voice that yelled, "FASTER, FASTER!!" And when you prayed "Now I lay me down to sleep" with me every night, my favorite part was hearing you say "forever and ever." Such a silly phrase, but all the more beautiful because it came from the mouth of the father I looked up to, speaking of a land that could surpass the unsurpassable wonders of forever. Forever AND EVER.

You encouraged me in every aspect of my life—artistic, musical, academic, social, and spiritual—always reminding me how beautiful, intelligent, and valuable I am. Even more than your encouragement and guidance were your actions, I remember comprehending at such a young age that you were transforming into a true man of God in front of my own eyes, with patience, discipline, and humility. Your embrace of my wild spirit and your honoring your own has guided me to love God wholeheartedly. This book is a testament to your lessons and love.

In our adventures, we touch the stars, the croc of time never catches us, and we outwit the pirate hood of adulthood. We are the lost children, now found in the Neverland of our dreams, forever young in spirit.

Context for Dad's Foreword

Dear Reader,

*Before you read the following foreword, I want to share some context. My father is not only an English professor with a remarkable 100% pass rate for his students, but also an exceptionally profound writer. He has founded multiple literary magazines, championed the wave of Freedom Writers for his high school students before the movie even came out, and has always been a step ahead of his time. As a secret pen writer, he has edited books for prestigious authors and been featured in numerous news articles. I could have easily asked him to write an extremely profound letter that would exalt me without a doubt. **However, the artist within me prefers this route, where the raw, intimate conversation between a father and his daughter remains.** Despite his many accolades, I chose to include this email he sent me in its original form to preserve its authenticity and heartfelt nature. His words are less formal but deeply meaningful, revealing the intimate bond between a father and his daughter.*

Tigress Weeps, Angels Dream

Forward by Dad

"

I often think of myself as Van Gogh-esque. Maybe that's why I like to paint like him. Never shall be understood. Truly. Always the outsider in some way. Seeing beauty always. Seeing the darkest dark - at times. Fighting to keep the mind even. I am pretty strong on that one. Like balancing on a surfboard for a long time. I have always set myself in an environment where I am safe and useful. Good lesson to learn.

I want to say that I feel so sorry for you that you had to experience such terrible evil at such a young age and be thrust into such an existential crisis. You are A VERY bright young woman. You are outcast because of this. Not only by them, but by being bright you just won't feel like you fit in. That's why you should hang out with bright people. You should probably work in a university. Keep this in mind. Your place is with bright people. They will understand your mind. Really. Most other people just won't click.

You are closest to all of my artistic, empathetic, idealistic, sensitive, genius self. So, God has a great plan for you. As long as you avoid the self-pity and nice dice due to realizing that a lot of the world is shit. And you don't really belong to it. But there are islands where you do belong. And you can launch boats to other misfits on other islands. And be their ferry.

Dad.

"

Author's note

Dear Reader,

The foreword that follows is a creative expression, written as if God is speaking to me. Inspired by scripture and my personal relationship with Him, it is not a literal letter from God, but a heartfelt conveyance of His love. I hope all the creatives and empaths reading it can also feel as though it's God intimately speaking to them as well as encouraging them on their journey.

Scripture References by order of appearance:

- *Psalm 119:73, Jeremiah 1:5, Isaiah 43:1,*
- *Psalm 139:14, Acts 9:15, Matthew 5:16,*
- *Ephesians 2:8-9, Hebrews 13:21, Ephesians 2:10,*
- *Matthew 5:15, John 15:16, Psalm 23:4,*
- *2 Corinthians 5:17, 2 Corinthians 3:3, Isaiah 50:4,*
- *Isaiah 51:16, Isaiah 43:10, Proverbs 3:5-6,*
- *Hebrews 13:5, 2 Corinthians 12:9, Jeremiah 31:3,*
- *Isaiah 60:1, Isaiah 61:2-3, Numbers 6:24-26*

✧ Forward by God ✧

My beloved child,

When I first created you, I did not merely make you; I fashioned you with the care and splendor of a garment woven with many colors. Before I formed you in the womb, I knew you, **Maranatha**. I have called you by name; you are mine. You are fearfully and wonderfully made.

You are My chosen instrument, **Maranatha**, to proclaim My wonders. Let the light of your words shine before others, that they may see your good deeds and glorify your Father in heaven. Your poetry is a testament to My grace, a reflection of My love. You are equipped with every good thing to do My will.

You are My masterpiece, **Maranatha**, created anew in Christ Jesus to do the good things I planned for you long ago. Use your gift of poetry to bring light to the world. Your words are like a lamp set on a stand, giving light to everyone in the house. Be confident, for I have chosen you to carry My message and to inspire others through your creation. Even though you walk through the darkest valley, you will fear no evil, for I am with you; My rod and My staff, they comfort you. You are a new creation; the old has gone, the new is here.

You are a letter from Christ, written not with ink but with the Spirit of the living God, not on tablets of stone but on tablets of human hearts. You have been given the tongue of those who are taught, that you may know how to sustain with a word those who are weary. I have put My words in your mouth and covered you with the shadow of My hand. You are My servant, whom I have chosen, that you may know and believe Me and understand that I am He.

Trust in Me with all your heart, and lean not on your own understanding; in all your ways submit to Me, and I will make your paths straight. I will never leave you nor forsake you. My grace is sufficient for you, for My power is made perfect in weakness. I have loved you with an everlasting love; I have drawn you with unfailing kindness.

Arise, shine, for your light has come, and the glory of the Lord rises upon you. Proclaim the year of the Lord's favor and the day of vengeance of our God; comfort all who mourn, and provide for those who grieve in Zion. **Maranatha**, may I bless you and keep you; may I make My face shine upon you and be gracious to you; may I turn My face toward you and give you peace.

With eternal love,

Your Eternal Father

Dedication

To my God, my eternal muse and guiding light, for inspiring these words and validating their worth.

To my family, the encouragers of my dreams and whisperers of wisdom.

To the friends I look up to.

To the unsung heroes—the everyday dreamers, the outcasts, the struggling artists, the single mothers, the young visionaries, the romantics, and the spiritual warriors. This book is a testament to your spirit. May these words be a beacon of hope, a sprinkle of stardust, and a reminder that art belongs to all of us.

And to myself, for dancing with the shadows, chasing the moonbeams, and never letting go of the light.

Contents

Seek and ye shall find.

◆

The pen is mightier than the sword

- Edward Bulwer-Lytton

Tigress Weeps

John 11:35

Isaiah 53:5 *(KJV)*

Isaiah 11:6-9

I seeked You all day
    I seeked You
even when I did not seek You
that invisible face of me
                    seeked You

when I opened
the door to the outside world
it was still, it was calm
it was blushing

my heart it **roared**

There Is Something in the Air

the universe is turning
the constellations are winking
the vision is within
   my reach
the eclipse is inside my mind
I am praying to You as if I'm
the sun, the earth, the moon
the moon has smiled & cried more
times
than I
this poem was written
deep within the scroll
before it was hidden in my
chest
all my desires are plain before You
bend Your tender ear, ear

These People Don't Care For Me

They are too, consumed by
their egos
they don't care, they don't care
I'm an ark, a rainbow in front of them
they did not walk beneath,
they walked on the other side
of the street
I've wrapped my pearls around their
head, a wreath
all they think
I do is speak
in the hands of a pauper
or a king
still, golden, am I

Refreshed I Am So Refreshed

I've hated me for my gift

I've been to hell & back

by no accident

because if God is in me

then every living thing

is beneath

which eyes see me?

send them to me

could I be seen?

which ears hear me?

mirror

in front of me

I see God within you

my garden retreat

Silence

my God I don't want to write
I'm not more clever than
any other. Who is listening to
me? is it You or I?
who needs to hear me is it
You or I?
who wants to hear me is it
You or I?
do I speak for vanity's
sake? or is it a release I
could never fathom.
in Your silence You keep me
You protect me
but I'm clawing out to hear
laughter of a friend.
Your silence is better than
all words of humans combined
a single word from Your **Word**
is better than any silence of mine.

did You curse me as a writer?
 no one sees these words but me.
did You curse me as a writer?
 to share these words is to
expose my
 wounds to the world
as they silently watch me
bleed.

Journey to the Stars

it is difficult for me to
speak the
language of the
heart.
if I speak
will it be heard?
or will I need to translate?
if I speak
will you see me?
or will I need to prove that my
softness
is not my fault?
if I speak
will you hear or will you listen?
will your heart respond?
or your carnal? or your mind?
or your instinct? or your heart? or your heart?
if I speak will you join me
on the journey
  to the stars?

wicked streets, fiery heart.

dart and swerve

boom crack bang

5 times in a row.

where am I now?

bet you wouldn't know

it's all passion

it's all zeal

arm up

stay protecting

my sacred heart.

in & out of battle

"**When we heal ourselves,
we heal the world.**"

..or so the new wave chants.

I cough up some blood
and spit it out
on this paper
and try at that chance.

Oh, I know I heal
when I speak from my truest heart.
And sometimes I don't even know the words..
until I see them present themselves,
as raw and purposeful
as many secret ancient martial arts.

My fist- My pain
My growl- My story
My speed- My determination
My wisdom- My healing glory

"When we heal ourselves,
we heal the world."

Yet, in my pain,
I fear my fears
of describing a blister to a babe.
How do I tell thee,
Fair eyes,
of the battles
I took the beat?.
How do I find the strength to
leak a breath of
my humiliating defeats?

Oh, the words I cringe, the words I hide,
Yet, the many ruined
ache to know…
of the virus that made me immune.
Of the phantom that made me glow.

you are so entrapped
  by your own misery
  swirling deeper into yourself
  without any means

the trees hum stories of gold from their green
woe, inside your home you grumble & groan
inside your triumphant heart
you scream

In My Own Hands
I died
and I did not miss her
she was ugly, she was hideous
in her last breath
no light left her
her death was torturous
her numb life, even more so
her hideousness was not her fault
so I pitying her and hated me for pitying her
I am happy she is gone
when memories of her come to me
I am not ashamed, she did the best
she could. She died in my arms
because I murdered her.

And my loneliness is set free
Never have I felt this way
And younger me wouldn't understand
But, friend, believe me when I profess
I find the most peace
within somber faces
the solemn ones
the masses
purposely evade
The faces that
look as though
they have seen what
no soul
could ever know
I feel them in my heart.
In my eyes,
gently,
I respond,
"me too".

it all makes sense now

God, help me be aware of all
the dots
signs and connections
like that of Orion, You put into place
no veil over this face
not a single thing of evil
will I lust for
You before ALL
even before my own
mane

Those stars!
wow, the multitude
there must be
more feelings
to experience, more
mysteries, epiphanies

taste the first round
life is wine
stick around friend, hero, star
you've turned your back
to your fears
not many see, I see,
you've stayed
sing,
I've renamed you
Unafraid

The best is nearly now,
it will be much better
than

on your own, on your
own
look into me a bit
longer, friend
stay for you
for me
sit with me, laugh with me
stay.
stay.

*inspired by Kayla
dedicated to anyone who has considered / or is considering suicide

Psalms

smile with me.
we dance palm in palm
under giant palms
believe, the trees have gentle eyes
they surely share secrets
of all of your splendor
as they, too, hold palms
and sing psalms down to their roots

The Friends of My Heart

O how I Love you
airplanes whirling
sparkles twirling
tell your story to me,
        O Storyteller.
feed me the bread
of your hearts
let it be warm
for it's your
character
that whirls & sparkles

Wind

the wind and I
are one and the
same
we both
know Your name
we both
know Your name

The spaces

between

You & I are

     infinite

You are always

     speaking

  to me

I am always

speaking

  to You

I am the mother, I am the daughter

I look Fear in the face
as though it were my mother
into those eyes that fear itself
    O how she really just wants us
    to be liberated
    and she does not know that
    that she does not know

May No One

not even your own

blood

take the elegance of

hope

from your

face

Your Success Will Ring in the Ears of People
Who Lost Hope in Their Own Souls

your success will change you
all will believe
that even a star
can be Jupiter
that even the depths of an atom
can surpass the limits of the speed
of light

~By the Fountains~

under the palms
reach out my hand to
the stars

I am bestowed
a paintbrush

Still
the night is still
comfort me
remind me
of Your promises comfort me
hello young star
did you cry into my
water?
hello little dreamer
a new day is dawning

Poetry Book

the moon shone in the night sky

in no metaphor

in no simile

the neighbors shared their cheesy

pizza

with the other neighbor

as I watched from afar

and smiled

I think myself a rising

The Poem of My Heart

the poem of my heart
my whole life I have been running from
my romance
but here I AM
the red rose of all red roses
here is my heart
the softest of all textures
at last
I AM both woman
and warrior of the heavens

I'm done running for
my life
I know a good song when I hear one
I see miracles everywhere
I know I am loved by God
I know that God sends me the
people that he loves
the fat of evil is slipping off of me
even in my stride
my legs are that of a horse's gallop
because You are my breath
not even my spine can hold me
upright
without You
selah

Grateful

I am so grateful

my gratitude knows no words

my gratitude is a new land

laid before me

Forgiveness

I forgive them all
for stumbling me
& feeding me lies
they wanted to watch me fall
&
burn
they did not realize
how much
You love me
how tightly You have
held on

Tigress Weeps, Angels Dream

your hatred
is yours
it does not belong to me

How can you love me
& not love my Spirit ?
how could you say
"there is a good thing there!"
then silence me
when I speak?
if I spoke of all the
gods
would I be worthy?
my house is warm
come in
the expressions on your face
might not mean a thing
still, your tongue sings in the
language of the heart

it feels so good to

believe in You

I was made to

believe in **You**

poetry is surely
not the thoughts
that come & go
poetry is the heart
that's sung in songs
never known

a true Artist does not need to
tell a story
a true Artist **IS** the story
     even their sigh is
the art

in the hollow of
the night
I was born again
a woman like any other
but my dreams were
      worlds
 and portals
tables where families were fed
laughed, looked at each other with a wink of a
smile
my God, made me so I might
dream, I've forgotten how to dream.
am I a warm dancing shadow of the night
as any warm dancing shadow
      ought to be?
I picked the flower with no
remorse

I wonder if my dreams ever
dream of me?

today I wiped my
tears with lavender
I didn't cut the stem
I said, "take these tears to God"

I believe they did

I don't know how
to love the places
and things You
give me
I want to love it but it slips
through my hands
a feather,
eternal water,
my child's laughter,
are the things that make me
glad
why am I here?
I don't understand?
how can I understand what I
don't understand that which
needs understanding?
where does the Milky Way
end and begin?
in a sea of stars
I only see a few outside my
window
but my faith can see them
dancing
in a dance my essence
remembers
this poem I have written it a
thousand times before
within Your mind
You birthed this world
did you not?
a thousand times because You
were sent and yet You began
and You are yet to come
a thousand times I have said
these words
a thousand times
that word is idle when it does
not belong to the throne of God.

if my love for
You be my
only fruit
then let
it be the sweetest

Wonder

don't withhold
Your wonder from
me
I wish to be in awe
to ruminate on Your word all
day long
and look into the might
of that thereof

my God, You rip-out
my heart and
reveal it in front of me
what a coward
what a shame
I rather fit in with man
even though Your
voice calls me
into the deep
forgive me
I renounce that part of
me
I don't know her
reveal to me who I really
am
even though I was a
coward
I have eyes to see
I have ears to hear
my gracious Father
let me try again

Dulce de Leche

You Lord of beauty

creator of beautiful

knower of beautiful

I wish to be more beautiful

beautiful in the way I listen

beautiful in the way I speak

make my face into water

my heart into my face

shower me

make my beauty that of
the most beautiful looking glass
so that those who gaze within
might see only their
perfections

make my words into the warmest
most impressive waterfall
so that the half-hearted
could believe in, You God, a gracious God
who wants us to be warm

Rock Stone

what's the point of this beautiful

face

if it does not confess the

beauty of my heart

the beauty of Your

heart within

my heart

rock stone was my pillow

I'm a beggar
asking for more grace
more grace
and I mean it
with all of my heart

If patience is the
          holiest thing I can
                    do
Then have Your hawk watch
me hold my daughter's hand
          and breathe every step
Your church was in my heart
                    today
But, my mind is far from it
          so I wept
          Today is the day of me
But, passing by a homeless
                    man
          there I am
          so I wept
The wildflowers smell like victory
My daughter gave them to me
          Is there a coincidence?
          There is none?

I don't care what
anyone says
I seek You because
I want You
My distress is not for nothing
Someone looked upon me in
prayer
they teared
because they saw You
I dusted my feet
I blessed the crooked
I don't belong on this earth
My soul is melting within me
My heart cries out to You
perpetually
It is torturous to be apart from
You
You hear me O you hear me O
that I know you hear me
A tigress I am here I take on a
pack of lions without fear
Yes, even in their hatred they
fear me
The eyes of frustration and
ignorance look upon me
past the brown into the eyes of fire
Savior O my Savior save We
I left the desert I was not
tempted
send Your angels,
strengthen me

Herald

when I think of
the herald of thy
face
I dive into those lips and
swim past the waters of you
    into the silver of my God
  you were wrapped in blankets
of my love
and then I undid you and let
    you twirl on your own and
pulled you into the sun
 of my God
where you twirled beyond my
vision into your own beauty
  I dreamt of you last night
and was ashamed of my love
for you because it was deeper than
 black and more wholesome than life
itself

who am I without my God
If my God tells me to forget you
I surely will
But if He tells me to pray
 at the feet of my God I will cry
 over the pink petals of your lips
cheetah, panther, tigress
on the hunt for the flesh of your pink petals
as the world laughs at
the crazy ones
    an Artist, I laugh
an Artist
I taste heartbeats, cry blood
vomit hallelujahs, the wildest of them all!

Night

it's the black of
the night
 the black of the night has
changed into a star
the stars into crystals
in the cavern of that star called night
that black night has left the
 sky
entered my heart
it goes on forever, I know
the curves
I've been there before
weeping diamonds
 that depth tells me I don't
have enough
that I'm not enough
it says "hold me" but it can't
 be held so who can hold it?
says I've nearly died of a
 broken heart
says give up on promises

speak to me as blue
 angels, aglow
with sweet words

 O heart how can I forget
that hope I love more than the landscape of my
pain

Time

time waits for no man
so I wait for time
because I am different
because I have been colored
outside the lines

Friend of Friends

I will not let
you slip
I will not let
you fall
can't you see?
can't you see them?
they're cheering
you on
angels even angels
archangels
cheer you
on & on & on
head up
you belong
shoulders back
stand strong

why have you
come to my
waters
why have you come
  why have you come
  to my waters
to my waters
to my waters
they reflect, reflect, reflect
they ripple
     they ripple
ripple, ripple, ripple
ripple, ripple
whatever lies I have convinced
myself
  I wish to forget them at once
what lies
have I told myself?
  where do they begin?
which one?
flee from me at once!
you know who you are
  at once, you know who you are.
I choose to believe in myself.

my God why is it
so hard to
maintain this
posture of humility
to hold it up
like it's dead weight to my
pride
when in truth it is my life
ever in humility
let it be a part of me
Your correction is not an arrow
past my ribs
through my flesh
it is a fire of refinement
so I might behold that
which can not be held back
when I correct my brothers
and sisters change my voice
into something greater
a dove
or a hand reaching out
to fingertips
drowning underwater
watch me, I walk on water

Sunflower Portal

I never knew
there could be a place beyond
the places I've known
the sunflowers smell so good
to me
You've made me into a bee
I don't want to go back
my thoughts are not my
thoughts
they are Your thoughts here
and I
just a portal
of flowers
an arc of flowers
no single flower was picked
here
they lived their day
when they fell, they told the
earth mercy as sweet
as my
lily hand
melting
melting
these thoughts are white butterflies
these dreams, the song of birds

Good Morning

the blinds to the
world of blue is broken
might we be grateful
when the blinds arise
will we thank our breath
and look the sun
in the eye?

Dance of Freedom

have you dreamt
of playing the harp of my
desires?
your voice is warm as sheepskin
your voice is as regal as a golden
scepter
all the other men are the ocean
you are a spring of drinking
water
all the other men are clouds
you are the stars of the night
all the other men are men
you are forbidden silk
you are forbidden gold
you are forbidden wine
you are forbidden laughter

Dance! Dance!

Dance with me!

The Love of Your Hands

hold my heart in
the love of Your hands
I can't know myself
until I know You
You made me in Your image
gave me hands
so I might wipe my own tears
so, tell me, did I wipe
my tears
or did You?
I wish man to love me
but he hates himself & his God
how can he love me?
if I skip a stone
what will make it float
science, faith, or mystery?
out of all stones
it is I, dancing on the many
waters of Your visage
which do I love more
Your mercy or Your grace?
Your mercy sings me good morning
"la los pajaritos cantan"
Your Rich Grace
tucks me in
with a kiss
"goodnight"

all day long I
 retreat into You
    they've raised my window

  still Your fresh grace
   is upon my face

 I want to lay in the grass of
 Your joy
 tell me I'm loved
 I will believe it!

"sit up, write,
you who hears my voice"
the fog of the dawn
-dimensions
are You the mountains of the earth?
or are You the mountains of the skies?
I wish to discover Your lands
so I might know my God
I wish to discover Your people
so I might know my God
call my name in every language
You are every instrument there is to dream

at once my
desires glue
themselves to
the floor
they do not desire what they
 once desired
they only desire You
You are King
King
King
King
I'll let you in my King
be nice
don't be cruel
You are my field of flowers

I have given up
all my dreams
my only dream
is You
I believe in You
as I believe in
the sun of the morning
the moon of the night
if You are my tea
let me be Your honey
from the white forest
of Brazil
give life to these words
of Love
breathe Your breath
into my story

You're on the tip

of my tongue

the tip of my paintbrush

the tip of my pen

my God

when he formed me

knew that I would love Him

before I could know that what

is Love

what is Love?

I wipe my tears upon Your robe
my feet are light
my alter is barren
though, I saw the
eyes of Jesus
in a man like
any other
feet upon a
satin embroidered cushion
eyes that have
escaped to the
expansiveness of
blue skies
could I know what
he knows of Peace?
what he knows?
a seed placed within
my chest
blooming pink petals
from my eyes
hold me. I feel alone
God is on my lips
before you go, bless me
he calls me Angela, by no mistake

my God, You
pummel me into
a pulp
whom shall I
fear? squeeze
me into juice
I'll go ahead
of Your people
in my shame,
You've hidden me.

perfect me!
only You can give
me the power
perfect me
only You can
straighten my eyes
perfect me
here, I don't deserve
what You have waiting for me
hide me however long, I'm obedient
the mountain is waiting
for your Word within me
the angels twirl upon the
"holy holy holy"
hide me however long,
even clouds must
obey at the rumble of
Your trumpet!
do not delay us
come swiftly!

in this lifetime

my soul tastes

redemption

in the air.

Visions

visions
I walk in visions
I am no accident
I AM who my God
wants me to be
"sit"
I am sitting
"dream"
I am dreaming
how could I sprint
from True Love's
destiny?

the world is being
swept away
by the sands
of fear
You, my God
are the Waters of
the Skies
a Blue Silk Drape
revealed before me
they ask how can I
see You
I respond
liberate yourself from
sin
God is both
miracles and the
trust within the fear
naked as the day I was
born before You
my hands are raised in worship
I know my God
when I see my God

there is a palace in Rome, laughter in
Morocco
I will not go
I will not go

I will only
go where You are

a shack in Pomona
if You are there
I will sit
I will meditate

even in the
hells of all hells

You are there!

I know Your

glory

like I know

my own tears

maybe, God,
You're not the places
nor the things
rather, the moments
amidst the places
beside the things
when I look into destruction I see
You
Lord is in my name
keep me uncomfortable
I crave what angels eat
manna
I cup open my
hands. I'm a beggar
feed me
in the night of myself
I've found You
You've been with me
all along
my arms are open wide

the things were just
things
   until I beheld
them
  then they each
turned into
    parts of God

watch me
transform
for You
love me as the
lovers love their wine
the poets love their creations
Divine
call me divine
pearls in my hair
I dream of angels
welcome me to the
realm of everlasting
clothe me in royalty
greet me with the
Son of Your
mourning
greet me with the
sun of Your
mourning, morning

others were
born in the house
of gladness. I was
born in the house of
mourning,
so love me
bless the neighbor
on either side of me
I too
have been blessed
You hear me,
a wolf howling at the
moon
darkness has
not consumed me

home

sling
10 wolf skins
upon this
burdened back
nothing can conceal this
lioness heart
that roars into the depths of the night
into the ears of wondering dream characters
hand over my heart as a pledged
with praises of love for my God
this passion can not be replicated
each word ornaments the robe of my Majesty
from Truth to Truth, Truth flutters home

This Morning

my children
were in the
womb of the sun

this morning God
birthed my
wishes
even before
the open of
mine eyes

I don't write my
poems to be
heard
nor seen
I write because
my words are
a baby bouncing
and these pages
are the mother
hold me

The Jewel of you

when you hold my
hand
it is the best thing
in the world
why would a dove
caress me?
why would a starlight
look up at me?
do you dream on me?
do I wish upon you?
or is our smile
a land of dreams come
true?
smile upon me once more
I don't need to wish
for a single thing more
my spirit's at peace
my heart's adorned

from the hierarchy
of the heavens
from the 24
elders
to the cherubim
I am just
a teardrop
I have been on
the cheek of

my Lord

the mirror of my soul
upon His cheek
only the children know
what the children know
only the faith-filled
know the secrets
of the fallen snow

Dream Interpretation:

I am chosen
admits Babylon I have eyes to
see God's glory & his grace
overflows
His grace is a precious river
I am an artist of God's word &
world
where others see gloom I see
truth & light
I rejoice in the children of God
Jesus is within me
men betray me and slander me
because I am blessed
angels are near to me
as close as a friend
I have found favor in my angel
God wants to increase me
add unto me
I am like the good shepherd
I go back for the lost sheep
I have the ability to favor
in the seat of the council,
God considers my voice

laughter fills my home
You are here,
my Lord
the cross is hidden
in my dreams for me
to find, You are here
my Lord
the lamppost is lit
among the moonshine's
last snowfall
Aslan is outside

waiting for me,
you are ever near
my Lord

my Jesus
how beautiful You are
my Shield
I can not contain
Your beauty
nor can I hold
it in
the snow falls all
around
Oh how I know my God
You're so easy to understand
You don't hide Yourself
from me
more I am ready
show me more..
more..more..

everything comes
and goes
but the disco ball
of Your splendor
lasts
Forever

Every Day I Wake Up

and I know who
my Savior is
to forget Your face in my
heart
is to forget the
blue of the sky,
to forget Your splendors
is to forget the smell
of a red briar rose,
to never have you
is a life
without the sigh
of poetry,
poetry is the curl in my hair
poetry is the monarch migration
within the park of
my mind!

Guava

I AM the rocks
at the base of the waterfall
of Your voice.
tell me Your dreams
for me
even the flowers have
their bees.

  help my wishes
wish for something greater
than I can taste
on the flower bed of
 my mind
if I AM the guava juice
who will gulp me down?
am I the promise
or the promise come true?
my tears hold the secrets
my flesh can not grasp
 my pen knows the answers
of my Spirit
to the questions
 my soul can not form.
if my heart was made
 of dust
why does it sing a song
of hope?
If hope is for the foolish
  why does it give me
life?

I am not the poems
I have written
I am all the poems
I have yet to write
neither am I poetry
I am a guitar in the hands of my

Beloved
falling in
love with
Us
as We play

I am not the poems
I have written
I am all the poems
I have yet to write

I am not the poems
I have written
I am all the poems
I have yet to write

I AM not the poems
I have written
I AM all the poems
yet to be written

I AM not the poems
I have written
nor AM I the poetry
yet to write
neither AM I poetry
a guitar is what
I am I am. is what I AM
in the hands of my Beloved
falling in love with Us as We play

write me into
existence
the gold ink
of the fountain
pen of Your sun
make me into
the expanse of Your blue
sky

materialize before me
my chin knows
the round of
my shoulder
anklets
toe rings
I carry breath
a vein ornament
within His
heart

tell me at once
world
tell me
who can love a poet!?
I am the caterpillar
I am the ugly duckling
 if you were blind
could you see my soul's face?
within the braille of these
words?
here is my soft pink mouth
here is my motherly breasts
here is my bloody heart
here is my laughter
 it fills the night
with a warmth of its own
there is a flower in my hair
there is usually always a
flower in my hair

I'm running away
as an act of
sitting on silk
from who I force me to be
into something more like the wind
something more like the kiss
on your lips
a memory yet to mold from the
clay of us
they cast me out
even though I'm sane
they made me feel
insane
wild even

yes, if I were shipwrecked on an
island I
would surely talk to myself
or the coconuts on the floor, wouldn't
you?

let us be as the
dragonflies
hold onto each other
as we fly
   gorgeous
today is gorgeous
in awe
every color of butterfly
has said hello to me
how can this be?
why me?

gorgeous

God, You are gorgeous

my love is a sparkling lake
ah, he will carry the
honeysuckle scent of me

invisible

even if You are invisible

my faith plays a sweet game

with the flesh of Your heart

Poetry whispers

itself to me

I've covered my ears

"I don't want to play
this game"

it tells me of a man as a *Hart*

behind the *trees*

of my love

who awaits me
"write me down"

"I don't want to play
this game"

you are the smell
of the most
handsome
cologne
I walk away
from...

how beautiful
that I
believe
in a Greatness
greater than
me

You are the only
conversation
worth having
the more I give of You
the more my chalice
overflows
You are the bread that
can be
divisible into forever
You are the crumb that
nourishes the bones

could my evolution
be beautiful?

from an alien
into a starlight of a babe

might I be your firstborn?

the one who teaches your
heart
a brand new love!
teach me how to walk
with patience, with patience
always with patience

then watch me
race into Your arms

and win the battles of
righteousness

YOU SPEAK
to me in my heart
I run
and play dead
as a coward
do I not realize
my life was made to end?
still I run and fool myself as if
there is any life worth living outside
of You
I believe in You with all my heart
while the people are filled with
doubts & debates
they need to hear in someone that
has no doubts in You whatsoever
no one can steal You from me
You are the Treasure of my heart
the Light of my lamp
the Covering over my head
I have made it through the nights of my despair, gasping
and gnashing for air
by the mercy of Your people, who also believe
in You, I am alive because You have saved me
through their hands, how selfish could I be to run
away from them & pretend that I don't want to
return
the favor & save them by Your word alone, my
gracious Lord of Lords, King of ALL Kings!

I am not the emotions
I am not the mind
   I am this moment
and in this moment
I am sweet
poetry

I don't want to be

    breath, bread nor bones

I wish to be poetry

    find me in the now

I will be waiting

basking

in the sun's light

a thousand birthday candles

and I

just a poem

of thanks

and praise

and awe

Friend

these words

a chandelier

these words

these words an angelic song

suddenly feel yourself whole

trust that in my eyes

your truest self

belongs

Ever

when you walk by my mind
one by one
all the flowers, all the flowers
bloom
bloom!

you are sun

you are moon

you are the peace
between salvation
and doom

Why Hide?

in a world of

lines + zombies

you are a cloud

how clever you are..

why hide?

my love for you

read your poetry

look off into the trees

the flowers

live forever

when they see your soul's face

Warmth

how favored
art thou
to pour
warm water

after warm water

feel the warm water with the back of thy
hand
like milk for a babe-
as light as a star.

know
it will always
be just
the right
temperature

claim thy
richness
that use to be
overlooked

my heart skips a beat

&

I am not afraid!!

You are a dimension
of angels
singing Your name
there is no I
how could I be sad?
when I am
within You
the experience of You
is my identity
I left the world
to follow You
remember me
birth me in Your realm
to be held in the arms of
my Salvation

I look so beautiful
when I listen to
Your voice
I'm a woman sitting in
Your
wind
holding the snake
it bit me and I did not
flinch nor
fade
I sit where the worriers
have
sat
more warrior that worrier
all sighs greet me
and walk away with praise

Favor

Your favor upon
me looks so
divine
it looks
like

breasts

that I love

Disbelief

I thank You, Lord

that even my disbelief

bows to You

Tigress Weeps, Angels Dream

And Jesus A Rose

I shall write
unto the Lord
until my
hand falls
off
God is stirring
in my heart
can't you
taste it?

As The Angels

I harken

unto Thy name

O Lord

"sit"

I shall

sit

"lay"

I will lay

I know all the pastures

by their name

anyway!

I acknowledge I am blind without
You
I acknowledge I am forgotten
without You
I acknowledge You are the key
to my sanity
I acknowledge You are the
mystery that makes me
exotic and mysterious
I acknowledge my most beautiful
words are still dust at the feet
of Your name
I acknowledge I am fearful
even when I convince my
body and tell it to be brave
everyday my tender feet
pray not to know the wrath
of Your anger
I acknowledge with You both
my heart's desires are answered
and my heart does not desire at all
I acknowledge with Your grace
and Your heart
I Love me all the more!

my Lord,

help me take ahold of my
thoughts
my thoughts are furious
stallions
without You
lead me to the land of You
could You glorify my soul
through Your Spirit
could I glorify Your Spirit
through my soul
though You are glory itself
without my hand
or my word
when my soul and Your Spirit
intertwine
I see us holding hands
less of hands
less of DNA
more of strands
red, burgundy, blue
curtains
coiled next to
the golden Ark of You
coiled next to
the golden Ark of You

Robe Me in Grace
if I were earth
Your grace would be
my clouds
if I were the ocean
Your grace would be
psychedelic fish
twirling

fishermen catch
me to eat me
to know me
to share me
long live Your grace
long live Your majesty

my love when I
kiss you
you will feel like
silk + velvet
at once I will coil my fingers
through your curls
+ they will feel as gold
my heart yearns for you
in the late-night
as a heart that has never
known fire
but can fathom a world
with the flame of a candlelight

do you not exist
if I have yet to hold you
or are you birthed in my
desires now
I must have already held you
for there is no barrier of time
that exists
within my God
and within my God
was always your love
the moment I was D.N.A.
a strand of hope
a breath a sigh
hear my sigh..

a butterfly

if I only live for a day
    would you love me all you can
if I only live for a day
        would you trust that your whole
life waiting
was worth it?

when you tear your tear
 my tear is in your tear
    that is why it is warm
for even there I hold you
 and if your tears go cold
        it is because your tears are in my tears
I've stolen you

Man

I keep running
into the wall of
man
I say, "Heart,
 be patient"
 yet, my Heart beats its beat
and it will continue to beat its beat
what does a heart know of
patience?
mine is made of the fabric
of dreams
where my true love's eyes
 will sing of seraphims
and a body that was once One
 come be One
again.

Can't you See It?

can't you see it?

can't you see it now?

when I love God

I love you

I write poems of my God

of my God of my God of my God

He's so otherworldly

His Love, divine

He made me

in all my **Disaster** He Loves

me

He has set me apart
He gives me the sweetest
dreams

Help

I ask for help
that's why Your people
want me to win
I know my privilege
that's why Your people
want me to win
when they turn away
I speak good things of them
they are a part of my blessings
they don't withhold the truth
from me
because they love me
and they know I can take it
when the sins of
Jealousy, Temptation, Anger
tell them to abandon or betray
me
they turn their backs to sin
because they see You
in me

The Lord's day is
brilliance upon me
it is a gown
it is my earrings
the red roses of my faith
do not fall
when His breath's upon me
a bull with wings
that is what
I AM
now watch me

fly

Call me the City of Righteousness
call me the Faithful City
Daughter Zion
I have fled to the
vineyards
I hide in a cucumber
field I learn to do right
justice is my
ribcage
righteousness is my nose
when I pray You look
upon me
even when I offer
many prayers
You listen
my new moon festivals
You delight in
my sabbaths You rest
beside me
the wine in my hand
is potent.
the silver within my pocket shines
I eat good things
of the land
the sword spares me
and considers my enemies

I hear Your
voice in my
chest
as a diamond
how beautiful
is Your voice
within me
I would be
nothing at all
without Your voice

in all of Heaven
in all of Earth
I have not
heard a name
more beautiful
than that
of my Savior's
every name of Yours just
a sparkle of Your majesty
Your hidden name
is surely hidden
in the center of the
New Earth of my heart

I can't get You
out of my head
so I invite You
within to sit
at the table

of my mind

there is nothing
I want more than
for You to return for me
the hearts of man
wither
before me
yet, the Lord will command
his lovingkindness
in the day time
and in the night
his song shall be with me
(Psalm 42:8)

what is Your song?
I know only a fingernail
of Your song
slingshot me, I'll be Your
shooting star in the skies
of You so I might hear you clearer
is Your song a voice like my own?
or a sigh of a non-believer who's changed their mind?

there is a stranger
around the corner
that needs me
they do not know me
but they need me
they do not know
the secrets that I know

Tigress Weeps, Angels Dream

Your goodness is so sweet
it is so pure it is so important
Your name is regal
Your name is written in gold
Your goodness sits me in the better chair
says I'm first
when I've been last my entire life
Your goodness loves me
more than I love me
because Your Love is the Truth of all truths
I've seen one shade of You
I've fallen in Love with that shade
don't show me more
You don't need to prove Yourself for me
I am completely convinced

when You speak to me
I am glad
when You are silent with me

I am glad

it is You I want.
not a single thing aside from that pasture of You
what rainbow? what crystal? which level of angels

can encompass that which is You?

what colorful bird? what word of love, of Love
can encompass that which is You?
roll me in the black of the night
I see stars no matter,
no matter!
I see those stars!

tell me of Your goodness

that unicorn horn is the heart of my brain
I have memorized Your splendors
as the poor man weeps
as the liar lies

the Lord is my Lord is my Lord is my

LORD

I hear Your voice
within the still of the night
the breath
of redemption
lacking, they call me worthless
plentiful, they call me
selfish
who knows these mysteries
other than my Lord
there is no relationship with God
only through the Son does he know
me
only through the Son do I know him
the heart of my Savior
is gentle & humble

I AM that sheep
he left the others to rescue
I AM that daughter
who came back home
to feast with my Lord, **my Lord!**

Angels Dream

Joel 2:28

Hebrews 13:2

◆

Revelation 19:10

◆

Famed Voices of Profound Wisdom

"Jesus was a man who was completely in touch with his soul. He was not afraid to show his vulnerability, and that is why he was so strong."
— Paulo Coelho (Author of *The Alchemist*, renowned for his spiritual and philosophical novels.)

"Jesus was not sent here to teach the people to build magnificent churches and temples amidst the cold wretched huts and dismal hovels. He came to make the human heart a temple, and the soul an altar, and the mind a priest."
— Kahlil Gibran, *The Treasured Writings of Kahlil Gibran* *(Author of The Prophet, celebrated for his poetic and mystical writings.)*

The Poet's Heart:
"I am a hole in a flute
That the Christ's breath moves through—
Listen to this
Music."
— Hafez, *The Gift* (translated by Daniel Ladinsky) (Beloved Persian poet, known for his lyrical poetry and spiritual themes)

"In the presence of Jesus, all doubts and fears are dispelled, and the soul finds its true home."
— Rumi (Beloved poet and Sufi mystic, renowned for his profound spiritual insights.)

"Stars shining bright above you,

Night breezes seem to whisper

'I love you.'"

— Fabian Andre, Wilbur Schwandt, and Gus Kahn, Dream a Little Dream of Me (1931)

Made in the USA
Las Vegas, NV
04 December 2024

a3e6b151-a5de-4715-8a58-472c0a601158R01

.